I Miss You, Delicate
Copyright © 2019 by Baruch Porras-Hernandez

Cover photograph by Mark McBeth // Used by permission

Author photograph by Fabian Echevarria

Cover design by Seth Pennington

All rights reserved. No part of this book may be reproduced or republished without written consent from the publisher, except by reviewers who may quote brief excerpts in connection with a review in a newspaper, magazine, or electronic publication; nor may any part of this book be reproduced, stored in a retrieval system, or transmitted in any form, or by any means be recorded without written consent of the publisher.

Sibling Rivalry Press, LLC
PO Box 26147
Little Rock, AR 72221

info@siblingrivalrypress.com

www.siblingrivalrypress.com

ISBN: 978-1-943977-60-4

By special invitation, this title is housed in the Rare Book and Special Collections Vault of the Library of Congress.

First Sibling Rivalry Press Edition, February 2019

I Miss You, Delicate

BARUCH PORRAS-HERNANDEZ

SIBLING RIVALRY PRESS
DISTURB / ENRAPTURE
LITTLE ROCK / ARKANSAS

for Victoria Hernandez

for Jose Porras

for Levi Porras-Hernandez

CONTENTS

My First Day of the Dead / 7

Things I've Never Done with Horses / 8

Matches   Maps / 9

The Sailor's Guide to Mermen / 13

Cloaked as Sparrows / 15

The Last Twelve Years at the Pueblo Near the Forest / 16

Tlaloc, El Llorón / 19

Templo de Humo / 20

Que Digan Que Estoy Dormido / 22

Eating Is Different / 24

Albany, California / 26

Double-Parked / 28

Paseo Tollocan / 30

We Shall Be Like Brothers / 31

The Dead Never Visit San Francisco / 34

Struts the Horse Remembers Mr. Hands / 35

Fog Song / 36

Missing Men / 37

The Last Day of the Dead / 39

MY FIRST DAY OF THE DEAD

There is a tombstone with my name on it.

One day I was taken to see it.
The cemetery is somewhere outside Toluca, Mexico.
My father and my uncles frantically cleaned it
as my grandmother swept around it.
My name is on that tombstone! I pointed out. I was four.
That is not you, my Uncle Paco said.
You're not putting me in there! I screamed, distraught,
fighting my first panic attack.
No, your uncle is in there! my Uncle David said.
My... uncle is in there? I was incredibly puzzled.
My grandmother stopped pulling weeds.
Your uncle is in heaven. Only his body is in there.
That didn't help. I was still very confused.
My father took me aside.
He was my little brother. He died right before you were born,
so we named you after him.
His name,   your name,   means
                              blessing.

I laid down on top of the grave,
pressed my face against the cold stone.
Closed my eyes.
When I opened them, my father, his three brothers
and my grandmother were all standing around me in a circle.
My father had the nervous smile he gets when I've done
something that embarrasses him.
I'm giving my uncle a hug! I explained.
Your kid is weird...
my Uncle Oscar said to my father.
Your kid is really weird.

THINGS I'VE NEVER DONE WITH HORSES

I have never ridden a horse to a lover's window
to serenade them in the middle of the night.
I have never robbed a train on horseback.
I have never taken a horse to water. I have
never horse-whispered. I have never
thrown a horse a birthday party.
I've never swam naked with a horse.
Annie Leibovitz didn't take pictures.
There is no coffee table picture book.
It's never been for sale. If a horse dies
I never beat it. I have never decapitated
a horse and left its head under the blankets
of my enemy while he sleeps. I have never
made love to a horse. My insides have
never burst from the penetration, causing
me to bleed to death, leaving an ex-wife
and kid. I have never been kept away
by wild horses. My great-grandmother
once fled on her fastest horse,
my grandmother wrapped
in her rebozo, a bloody feud
behind her, she took refuge
in a town that later became
the city I was born in.
I have never looked into the
giant eye of a horse and not
been reminded of how fragile
humans are. How powerful
we must have felt,
riding beasts that once
helped us create the world.

MATCHES   MAPS

Learn how to grow and store your own food Bud tells me.
He is the oldest, most intelligent gay man I know.
He's heading for the hills.   *My generation didn't do enough*
he says   *All that work.*   Every weekend he takes supplies
to a cabin deep in the woods. No one knows where it is.
Are you and your partner prepared? he asks. *For when it comes?*
I look at the cold water of the bay, how green it is.
No, I say, *we're not.*

My partner turns his body away from me.
    He doesn't talk.   He lies in the bed   not sleeping.
Tells me not to touch him.   Demands I give him space.
      We live in a fucking studio.
  I take my laptop to the bathroom,
sit with it in the bathtub during a thunderstorm.

    He comes in to pee.

  He goes to work.
      He comes home   lies down
         turns his body away from me.

My friend Joey invites me out for a drink,
tells me he is HIV positive. He is 24. We sit at a bar
in the Castro lit by Christmas lights. The waitress brings us whiskey.
I squeeze his little hands. Our tears flow freely.
Men wearing Santa hats outside sing Christmas carols.
There are Santa Drag Queens everywhere.
I want to burn the Castro down but he says
I'm happy to be alive.   *I am grateful for every single day.*

I had a car once, a blue Oldsmobile, with a white leather top
that would break down on me once a week, twice a week sometimes,

always in large stretches of highway in the middle of the night
before cell phones   so I walked to the nearest
middle-of-nowhere payphone and so
my father would drive into the night
searching for me through the fog,
teaching me to forgive on dark California highways.
Remember, always call me when there is an emergency, he would say,
No matter where I am. I will always find my way to you.

When it comes, you and your partner will be isolated
Bud tells me as he packs more supplies into his truck.
No one will be allowed on the bridges,
no one will be allowed on BART, be prepared, make sure you have a radio,
make sure you have a meeting point, have a plan. If there is a tsunami,
or war, or something else comes from God-knows-where to cut us down again
by the thousands, or   an earthquake or everything falls apart,
if you and your partner are in different spots of the city,
how will you find each other?

I keep peering into the windows
of the houses I pass by as I walk after work.
I wonder if they're prepared? I wonder if they're prepared?
They're probably prepared, look at that house,
all that fucking money, they will most likely survive. They are prepared!
As I walk, I wonder if my partner and I would fight less
if we had a living room
if we had a couch.   His eyes
green butterflies   smile at me.   I turn away
from him, stare at the large window next to our bed,
wonder if it will break over us   when it comes?

Joey tells me I was there the night he was infected,
picked up by a man who wouldn't look me in the eyes.

Don't go with him I told him. *Don't patronize me*, he said,
I am an adult, I'll be fine, I can take care of myself.
I grasp his tiny hands. *Call me if you change your mind!* I begged.
Call if anything happens. I will find my way to you. Later the man
thrust his face against a shower wall. Joey woke up
in a hotel hallway, then spent the night walking the streets
of San Francisco waiting for the trains to start running again
and take him home.

My father says *I wish you didn't live in that city,*
your neighborhood is so dangerous, be cautious where you wander at night,

I did not protect you, when you were young, forgive me
my father says as he drives me back to San Francisco,
he didn't tell me about the nightmares
    I have nightmares,   *that you get attacked*   *men, beat you to a pulp,*
       and I can't do anything to help you   *till years later.*

Should it break, should it all go to hell, find your way up north,
don't take a car, walk through the forests, take this envelope,
don't open it until it all goes to shit, inside, there is a map
find your way to me.

I just don't want to talk about anything, that kills you doesn't it?
That kills you doesn't it?

At one point I just wanted to have enough money to settle all my bills
and debts so that I could die but now I'm here
with you healthy and alive! I am going to live for a long time
and I'm grateful for our friendship.

Wake up, I've stopped the car, open your door
and get out, look, look there, look, surrounding
the city, a white impenetrable wall of fog
before us, welcoming you home.

Do not pace at night, blaming yourself, when you can't sleep,
it is not your fault what happened to me.

He hums to himself in the kitchen,
while I fold our laundry on our bed.
He comes into the room, kisses me on the cheek.
He is in a good mood. *Are you leaving me?* I ask him.
Before he can answer, a siren screams throughout
San Francisco. We both look out the window. We wait
to hear for the voice to tell us that it is only a test.
Is it Tuesday? he asks.   We wait.

Bud tells me *water never came to wash people's homes away,*
when I was young...   I knelt under desks,
dodged drafts   police batons   even AIDS,
watched so many of my brothers die   but the earth
was not falling apart   back then,
Bud tells me *learn how to use tools   and guns,*
keep water in jars   keep matches   and maps,
know the roads   know the back ways,
but most importantly   stock up on flashlights.

   One day,
you may need to feel safe as you walk through the dark,
    searching for the men who once held you
       in the pitch
         of midnight.

THE SAILOR'S GUIDE TO MERMEN

Contrary to ancient myth, Mermen do not sing.
They write sonnets with their ink, stuff them into bottles
that wash up on shore. If a bottle touches your feet,
leave it on the beach, for their words sink into your skin,
fill your mind with answerless riddles, give your body
a fever only the sea can break. You will find yourself
walking towards the ocean in the middle of the night,
see the Merman's glowing green eyes waiting for you
through the waves. You will find yourself
in the Merman's arms, head barely above water.
He will whisper in your ear

Take me with you, breather of air, and I will love you more than the sea,
   take me with you, cut my hair,   and it will set me free.

No matter how beautiful he is, do not go home to
get a pair of scissors, do not kiss him after cutting
his long green seashelled hair, for in the moonlight
you will have to listen to his screams as his fins
split in two, watch him writhe in pain as they form
into legs. Whatever you do, do not spend the night
licking the salt from his skin, do not make love to him
on the sand, do not let him hear how humans moan,
for he will follow you home, call to you as you walk
away *I did this for you! I did this for you!* If you walk faster,
he will learn how to run. If you run, he will call out
your name in the dark. Do not lead him to your door.
Do not let him in.

After a couple of days, you may notice
that the sunlight slowly turns his green skin
pink. To keep him from having nightmares,
leave a glass of salt water by his side of the bed.

Make him wear clothes. This will keep you from
becoming obsessed, keep you from taking him
every minute of every hour of the day, so much
that you will start losing sleep, stop going to work,
forget to eat, forget to drink. Do not let him
use your blood for ink. If he asks you to hold
his head under water in the bathtub or the sink
do not let him call it love. Whatever you do,
do not fall in love.

Do not panic when you wake with a mouthful of mud
to find he is dragging you back to the sea. There is no
way to break the Merman's spell. Now, you can plunge
a blade into your heart, bathe his feet with your blood
turning them back into fins to set him free, or you can
let him drag you into the water, hold your lover as you
feel the water rise over your head, let him whisper in
your ear as you both drown,

There's nothing to fear,   come with me,   come with me,
   into the darkness of the deep   come with me,   come with me
    I love you, ever more   than the sea.

CLOAKED AS SPARROWS

When they came for me, putting my hands together didn't do any good. Neither did acting like a bird or pretending to fly. They still took my eyes. They call themselves Angels, cloak themselves as sparrows, imitate doves and terns, hunch over like crows, tell everyone they know how to fly, but no one has seen them do it since no one has eyes. They call themselves storytellers, swooped into libraries, destroyed books, stormed into schools perched on children's shoulders, stabbed little ears, deeper and deeper, till brains were picked out, wriggling little pieces from skulls like worms in their beaks, covered children with feathers, placed them atop buildings, commanded them to fly. When I saw my friends leap from buildings, I tried to cover myself in feathers, tried to act like a crow, tried to peck at the ground, but they still came. I didn't put up a good fight. There was nowhere to run. I tried to hide in a phone booth, the last one on the motherfucking face of the motherfucking world, but they surrounded me, threw themselves at the booth, until they broke through. I was forced to bob up and down, broke my nose against the concrete floor, then they covered it with a beak. I was feathered from head to toe as they held me down to peck out my eyes. A scream came from my mouth. They all made noise with me, mocking, imitating, then I stopped. Everything was dark,
   but they kept going
      How beautiful we sound! they cried.
        Welcome, fellow songbird! they said,
           some of them.

THE LAST TWELVE YEARS AT
THE PUEBLO NEAR THE FOREST

When I got to the barn   my son's body dropped to the ground
meat from his neck still in the monster's jaws   blood oozed
from the monster's mouth to the scream coming from my son's
open throat   I called to the monster   *You are a man! A man!*
You are not a monster! as it crawled slowly over to me   eyes glowing
my hands shaking   voice trembling   *You are not a monster!* I cried
Your name is Olmo.   Olmo!   Olmo,   stand up,   stand up,
wipe the blood from your mouth.   It slowly stood   its eyes
fixed on my pitchfork   and breathed   the more I called him Olmo
the more he became Olmo   the more I called him Olmo
the more the black mane fell away to show pale cold skin   yellow eyes
turned blue   *Your name is Olmo* I said   Olmo repeated   *Yes*
Turn around Olmo I said   and we wept   and wept
me over my son's broken body   Olmo in the corner covering his face.
I grabbed Olmo by the hair   pulled him to where my son
laid in a pool of blood   forced him to look at what he had done.
Olmo howled and screamed   but it did not match my own   or my wife's
or my oldest son   or my daughters   all ready to take Olmo's life.

When el pueblo heard, they brought torches, rope, swords, whips,
but I stopped them at my door. When I spoke I felt a long, high-pitched
moan coming from my throat like a dog not being able to let himself
howl at the moon, but I held back, and walked, every step
more painful than every last breath ripping through my chest
I dug into my body to find more sorrow and sorrow, and
after I put my wife, my daughters to bed,
I put Olmo to work in the shed.

My oldest son, furious and mad, attempted to kill Olmo in the morning,
afternoons, late at night. I stopped him every single time.
      Gave Olmo a cot to sleep,   a bite to eat,
          gave Olmo water, a towel, and a rag,   and in the morning,

I gave him a shovel, and we walked to the woods, there
he dug a grave for my boy, then we walked back to the house,
where my family prepared the body,

then the march through the town,
full of more pain,   so I floated into the air,   inexplicably,
floating to watch my old, aged face, shrunken body, walk next
to the young men carrying the body of my boy.
I laid myself on top of the screams of the wailing women,
I stood on the head   of Olmo who led the way
      and so we laid the dead flesh to rest
and the priest did what he did, said what he felt he had to say,
my wife slapped Olmo   across the face, spit in his eyes,
the whole pueblo turning away, the judge,
pointing the finger at the terrible man demanding Olmo's head.
The old men screamed, threw rocks at his head.
He, so horrified with what he had done, let the rocks hit his face
let my wife's hands scratch his chest. My oldest son
pulled at his ears and screamed.
I shot my gun into the air, pulled the crowd off of Olmo,
walked him back to the farm
where he worked for the next 12 years.
One for each of my son's life.
In the mornings I would say to his face   *You are not a monster,*
your name is Olmo.   After there was no work to be done,
he would fix things in the pueblo, help old people with their troubles,
helped build the dam, cut firewood, build houses, cribs.
He also dug more graves.
One night, as he was preparing his cot on the grass, near a tree
that watches over my house, I forgot to tell him he was not a monster.
In the morning when he licked his lips, as my youngest son walked by,
without thinking, in a second, I shot Olmo, right in the back of the head,

not knowing I was capable of taking a life. Olmo's head, the pieces
floated into the air, I tasted the heat of his blood, his brain spraying
on my shirt that was shrinking way too tight.
I felt my back break into a hunch. I felt the air flow out of me,
watched my fingers turn into claws   my teeth began to cut my tongue,
    in horror
I watched my body begin to slowly grow razor-sharp deep black hair.
My oldest daughter, who had heard the gunshot,
came running out of the house, stopped
dead in her tracks, horrified by my transformation,
Hija! Hija! Don't be alarmed! It's me! come closer! come closer!
it is your father, no, don't scream! Don't scream!
I am not a monster, I am not a monster! Quick, before it is too late!
Tell me my name!   Hija!   Call me by my name!
    Dime que no soy un monstruo!

TLALOC, EL LLORÓN

In 2011 approximately 40,000 people were killed in Mexico's drug war.
Most received a bullet to the back of the head.

Tlaloc was the Mexican/Aztec god of fertility, rain, and water.

Things change.

When the men open their eyes
even the blood looks deep blue
against their shirts and coats.

Each man holds a bullet in his teeth. Their march,
in straight lines on either side of the road,
at first seems endless but then they see the lights.

The last town, when the men reach it, their hair wet,
bodies cold, still, they take off their clothes. Leave them
in neat piles in front of doorways, on windowsills.

They fall to the ground,
miles and miles of moving backs
naked men, crawling towards the last river

where the weeping man waits. Once
the god of fertility and rain, now El Llorón kneels,
one leg in the mud, one in the water,

a giant, the largest being the men of the earth
have ever seen. One by one, he picks up the dead men like cats,
kisses them on the mouth, sucks out the bullet that killed them,

cradles each man in his arms,
rocks them slowly into little sleeping balls
then gently places them in the last river to float downstream,

and into the next realm of the dead.

TEMPLO DE HUMO

There is a room made of cigarette smoke
The men enter   She sits chain smoking
She opens her mouth   and brings them back to life
then bites out their throats   swallows them whole
walks to a corner   shits them out
Sacrifice   How she missed it   for centuries
She screams   *I will never weep again! Not for the rest of the eternity!*
Mis hijos? Ay   they can all go fuck themselves!
more men enter the temple   on their knees
they ask for the Virgin   beg for forgiveness
she opens her mouth   brings them back to life
says *no   I don't forgive you*
then goes for the throat

    The other gods left! Only some of us stayed
    I transformed myself into a Virgin para qué? para qué?
    for mountains of red flesh shaped like sleeping women?
    these men   I will devour them over and over again
    until the end of this realm!   Then I might join the others
    but there will be more
    They keep coming to me on their knees
       Good   I hunger
    They forget I was once the goddess of death as well
    I should have never learned Spanish!
    I barely speak English! para qué? For fucking what?
Another man enters the room made of cigarette smoke
He is scared   She pulls back her hair

        Two snakes twist
        They form a smile

    She shows him her earrings
    made out of las manos de un hombre
      aren't they adorable   te gustan?

Outside the temple made of cigarette smoke on Tepeyac
where she first appeared to Juan Diego back in 1531
There are so many spirits of murderous men
that they form a line   wrapping around the temple
in circles   most of them wait patiently sitting on the ground
    Drops of rain begin to fall
    There is a great flood coming
        The men look up   open their mouths.

*Coatlicue, mother goddess of life and death, transformed
into la Virgen de Guadalupe.   Now she eats.*

QUE DIGAN QUE ESTOY DORMIDO

The fires lasted 289 years   the spark
from the last Mexican   to ever light a cigarette
   set them aflame

scientists, perplexed   study the enormous smoking mark
on the earth   where   Mexico used to be
you can see the mermaid-shaped burn from space

No gods fled this time

No deities hid behind virgin veils
but drug lords cried their little hearts out
their bellies grew   so large   when they burst
rivers of blood and gasoline flooded every city

        we are all just sleeping.

the women
chased the men to the mountaintops
sacrificed them   showed the sun
the beating muscles but still   night came
the women threw the bodies from the cliffs
lit torches   knelt   let snow slowly cover them till they became
lumbering volcanoes   singeing the belly of heaven

        let them say we're sleeping
cradling each other   like brothers   backs to guts
   guts to backs
bullets   buried in the ground
still taste us in their blossoming mouths

we are   ashes   lying still on the ocean floor
resting in the pockets of lungs   children
try to brush us from their teeth   we live
under fingernails
    we don't disappear
    no Mexican ever does
    let them say we're sleeping
    we are all just sleeping
    waiting   to be buried
     in a place   no one
      can ever
        return to.

EATING IS DIFFERENT

you are no longer 12
    you have done the most treacherous thing
    you are different, they scream
    this isn't you! you are different!
    you are different!

dinner is different
    the chairs are positioned differently at the dinner table
    you chew a little slower, your family looks down
    when your father turns on the small television
    and begins watching the news, your mother doesn't say
    turn it off, this is family time. She looks at her food,
    then at you
    and quickly turns to the news to silently watch.

driving is different
    quiet, no music in the car or fighting or arguing
    unusual for a Mexican family
    when you stop, you stay in the car, all you can do is wait
    when people ask why you stay in the car
    your parents simply say *He's not having a good day.*

church, family outings, get-togethers with friends are also different
    you are the last to be introduced
    no longer encouraged to mingle
    your parents no longer mind if you sit outside.

weddings are different
    you stay at the table, your parents get up and dance
    though they have not danced since their own wedding
    they drink, though they do not drink
    hold each other close,

during a slow song your mother looks at you,
her head resting on your father's shoulder,
then shuts her eyes.

you don't pray
did your face burn when the police officer took your picture?
your mother's voice is different
her movements are different.

night is different
your mother walks by your room
stops at your door, your lights are out
she looks down
after a moment she mutters *You are not alone*
then walks away.

ALBANY, CALIFORNIA

Go down head first   on your back
watch the sky circle   spin.
Run away.
When you find you can't go past
San Pablo Avenue   go home.
Get a boner for every guy
who doesn't beat you up.
Get a boner   for every guy who tries.
Run away.
Get lost in Emeryville.   When you
run out of money and out of ideas
                     go home.
Walk silently past the tiny bars,   memorize
all the little houses trying to be castles.
Look at the white giant glowing cross
on the hill,   hear the rumors of the monkey
that lives in the trees, the satanic cult sacrifices,
believe   every   single   rumor that touches your ear.
Know everything there is to know.
Tethered only by street lamps   walk far
with your friends   in the dark.
Prepare yourselves   to finally,
truly   see.
Make a pact
to not come back   grown empty
heavy-legged men.
After the sunrise   continue the endless
walks home.

When your parents fall apart
stop running away.
Slowly   learn what the world is,
but keep your belief in good things.

Discover what a guy's body tastes like.
Fall in love.

For the last time   before they take it down
climb the 30-foot-orange-twisting slide.
Spend the night up at the top.
In the morning,
stare out into the white gray sky,
   then let your body
      fall down   in circles.

DOUBLE-PARKED

Night ends   you are double parked
in front of your house in your father's truck.
He had shown up to your reading at the bookstore
in a suit. The other gay men there said he was very handsome
for a man his age. *muy guapo, dios mío,*
then he gives you a ride home to the city,
all the way from Berkeley.
Before you exit his truck,
he recites a poem he wrote about you when you were five years old.
He never shared it with you because he thought
filling you with poetry would make you weak.
You know it by heart? you ask him. *Of course I do,* he says,
I know all the poems I've written to you by heart.
My favorite I wrote to you is called "Little Soldier,"
because you always stood so tall, always protected your mother,
like it was the most important, noble thing to do,
you protected her from everything and everyone,
even from me.

My father says I used to give him time-outs
when I was four. He reminds me I used to call him
into his study to reprimand him for his behavior.
We're still double-parked in his truck in front of
my place on South Van Ness and 23rd. My father tells me
I used to point my small fingers at him and say
I don't want you treat my mother that way, ever again
then I would dismiss him so I could go play.
I do vaguely remember doing that.

Before I leave to go up to my apartment,
he tells me not being with my mother is like a bleeding wound
that will never heal.

I say *Dad, that is an overused terrible metaphor.*
He laughs. *It's true though*, he says.
I say, *you better get used to bleeding then.*

I tell my father to become comfortable with the loss of blood.
That I hope he can keep himself up and is able to walk.
Losing blood makes you dizzy. I tell him to drink lots of water.
*Take a hot poker, Dad, put it to that wound, hold it there till it is black
and the smoke fills your nostrils, hold it there till you can
no longer feel anything there at all, then learn to love the scar.*

    Treat it better than you treated my mother.

PASEO TOLLOCAN

In my dreams I have floated, and I have fallen,
but I have never flown.

Both my parents have had dreams about flying.

My mother once told me that she used to go
jogging with my father along a part of town called
Paseo Tollocan in Toluca, Mexico,
the city where I was born.
He would always run faster than her
and laugh when she'd try to keep up. She tells me
that one day, his mocking infuriated her so much that
she cleared her mind, concentrated, got faster,
then faster, caught up to him, and passed him.

No matter how hard he tried, he could not catch up.
Shocked, flabbergasted, and finally out of breath,
he began to curse at her as she kept going
till she couldn't hear him at all.

She said that night she dreamed that same scene except
that she not only passed him, she flew up into the air.

It was exhilarating   she told me   *feeling your body*
fly through the wind. I looked down. Your father
got smaller and smaller,
till I could no longer see him.
She tells me that in the dream
she felt completely free. She had never felt truly free.

All I kept thinking was he can't reach me!

                From up here,   *he can never reach me!*

WE SHALL BE LIKE BROTHERS

My brother is 4
I tell him—I'm going to put this blanket over your head, and when I do, you'll be transported to another dimension. I'm really sorry. You won't be able to come back. It was nice knowing you. Instead of panicking, he takes a deep breath grabs his favorite bear, puts on his serious face, says—Tell mom I said goodbye. Then lets me put the blanket on top of him.

My brother is 21
I tell him this is not his last broken heart.
When he asks me why? I tell him
—Because life always gives you at least two.

My brother is 5
We drop him off at preschool for the first time and the whole family is worried. He doesn't speak English yet. Later we pick him up, ask the preschool teacher how his day was. If he was okay. She says—Oh, you mean the ladies' man? YEAH! He's OK! Been walking around surrounded by five ladies all day! My little brother is escorted to the door by five little girls who all kiss him goodbye then run back to the playground. He keeps a serious face during each kiss. In the car, my mother asks who those girls were? My brother quietly says—My girlfriends. My mother looks worried. We head towards our house. My father silently driving does not hide his giant smile.

My brother is 18
Tells me he doesn't want to be a weak person. I say—You are not a weak person! Eres el más fuerte y el más cabrón que conozco! After I was born, our mother was told she would never have children but then she had you. You were born so big and so strong the doctors and nurses stood in a line to take turns holding you. You are strong, still. Stronger than all of us.

My brother is 22
He wants me to help him write a short story. I say of course. In the middle of it, he gets frustrated, wants to quit. Tells me—You got mom and dad's writer genes, I didn't. I say—Well, don't be too sore. You did get the better ass, and the good heart. You got the good heart.

My brother is 6
I go through the most traumatizing part of my life. He is the only person that never calls me a monster.

My brother is 19
He says—This country won! We lost! I'm here in Davis, by myself, you're in San Francisco, alone. Our mother grows old, at her house, alone! And our father is off in his apartment probably falling asleep on his couch by himself. I tell him there will be a day when each of us will have someone to come home to. He says—Immigrant stories are not supposed to end up this way. We should be coming home to each other.

My brother is 23
The woman he loves, he fears, has stopped loving him.—I don't want to give up—he says —I want to fight for us, I don't want to give up, I don't want to give up. What do you do when you feel like the world is moving too fast and you've been knocked off and are floating away? I tell him—I throw the covers over my entire body till I can't see a peep of the outside world. My brother crawls onto my bed, begs me to make him disappear again. I pull the entire blanket over him.

Hermano
I'm going to pull this blanket off from your head, and when I do, you and I will be grown men. We will no longer live in Albany.

Mom and dad will be old, divorced.
Everything will not be the way it should be
but you and I
walk this new terrible world, finally
like brothers.

My brother is 4
I pull the blanket off from his head. He looks at our backyard like it is a new world. Walks around slowly blinking, observing, pulls the grass, touches a leaf in the bushes like it is the first time he has ever touched one. Transformed into an explorer, he keeps walking out of the backyard, begins crossing the street,

I run after him.

THE DEAD NEVER VISIT SAN FRANCISCO

Instead, they ride the fog
to the Golden Gate Bridge
where they sit on the cables
to watch the sunset.
After, they keep their dead eyes
on the waves
and wait.
When it is fully dark
one by one
the jumpers
poke their heads out of their grave,
float back on to the silent, steel
stare out across the bay,
      then let themselves fall
      all over again.
The spirits of the city
try to stop them,
Come with us, to the next world
they beg,
an invisible battle
no one can ever see
as cars rush by.
Each year, some suicide ghosts
decide to leave with the others,
to finally rest.
      Most of them
jump again,
back down,
sink to the bottom of the waters
to wait,
for the next Day of the Dead.

STRUTS THE HORSE REMEMBERS MR. HANDS

So they could sleep at night, they took me far away from
the farm after you died. When they searched the house, they found
the cast of my cock you made while I was perfectly erect. To quell
their fears of ending up the way you did, I was left as empty as our
red barn sits now.

I miss you, delicate.

I miss you pressed against my side, your hands on the ground,
waiting for me.

I think often of the stories you told me. Of the glorious young man
who dreamt of feathers, taken to the sky, caressed forever, wings,
claws ripping into blushing skin. Of the girl and the swan, apples
split open, fir trees, weeping willows, panting in the morning air,
how she opened her legs to the bird.

There is a blind horse at this new farm where they keep me. It is
fed well, yet it searches the blackberry bushes, hoping for sweet,
repeatedly stabbing its eyes with thorns. Berry juice and blood drip
down its sides; it is a painting of you and I.

At night, I dream I didn't kill you. You are young.
I am a small cow. You take me to a river, hold my head under water
until I drown. Then you kill yourself so we can be together forever.

Then I wake up. You are still gone, and I am alone,
weeping for the day
I can beg you to forgive me.

FOG SONG

When the first people that ever stepped foot
onto what is now called San Francisco arrived,
I welcomed them with a cold, wet kiss. Rolled
over the hills and sand dunes, rested softly
on their heads, circled their feet. I became so thick
they couldn't see their hands, made them feel
like they had disappeared. I still love making
the temperature drop, clasping my hands over the sun,
laughing as people hopeful for summer hug themselves,
protecting their nipples from me. They go home,
come back warmer dressed, light a cigarette
and walk around smoking in my drizzle.
Children run around in the city at night,
weave through street people as if they are trees
jump over the sleeping bodies on sidewalks,
mothers walk slowly after the buses stop running
as they pray, I slowly follow them. People,
I remember them before they built the buildings
and roads. See the young ones pressing their gadgets
and phones, just like fingers once pressed into
sieves, searching, working, thirsty for gold.
When I lay myself on top of this almost-island
I give them a message of things to come.
Not earthquakes, or fires, or waves from the sea,
but the cold. The cold is coming. One day,
a great change will bring an endless frost,
cover the city with snow, turn its hills into
pillars of ice, and the last people to ever leave
the most beautiful city in the world will carry it
in their chests, glowing like lanterns
When that time comes, I will become heavy.
I will become homesickness, follow them
everywhere they go, a reminder of the place,
where they found their hearts.

MISSING MEN

All of the men who once held you
     are gone from the world.
  You keep water in jars.

You stocked up on flashlights.   On the trail
you listen for your father's voice   the way it sounded
before cellphones.   You remember
on dark California highways
the way your father's headlights cut through the fog
    You find   old middle-of-nowhere payphones
walk past broken down cars.   You wish you had
   your father's nightmare eyes.   See men
with skulls cracked open   blood on the sidewalk
reflecting the street lights   that   are still   lit.
You think of the recurring dream your father
never told you about   till years later.
     You wonder where he is   now
       as you walk.

Your friend Joey disappeared.   You carry matches,
walk in circles around Union Square
above the sleeping BART trains.   Looking for the man
that didn't look you in the eyes.
You walk past the bar Twin Peaks.   You look for whiskey
but the lights are all out   the streets   hug empty buildings
that were once full of men.   You hear Joey's voice.
You remember his tiny hands.   The flag is gone
        the flag is gone   for
the earth shook   opened
   swallowed all of the men into the ground.
    You learned to grow your own food.

You look in each hole   to see which one
your partner might have fallen into.   You two
were a window   shattering   raining glass.
You two were a tiny studio that wished
it had a living room   someday   someday
but until then   you two
were an old building crumbling down.
When everything fell apart you two
were on separate ends of the city.
            His eyes
were the color   of the   cold green bay.
            You had no emergency plan.

Bud   your oldest gay friend   changed one day.
Gave you an envelope   there is a map in it
    to a place   in the woods.
Each weekend   he was taking supplies up there
    no one knows where it is.
Bud said   *When everything turns to shit*
    find your way to me.
            Now he's gone.
You open the envelope.

You gather your guns   your matches

your flashlights
        your maps   your water in jars

        and you walk into the dark

with nothing
            but the cruelest part of the night

            holding you close.

THE LAST DAY OF THE DEAD

my mother will not celebrate day of the dead
as a child
she believed she could tell   when people were going to die
then they would die   and she would see them   again
a lot of them don't wait for day of the dead   as a child
head under her pillow to drown out their sounds   at night
when they visited   they were loud   strong   ate the most food
burped for fun   not just humans   my mother
saw birds   pecking the ears of her cat Pepino   swirling above

today   when I ask my mother why she doesn't celebrate it

she says
if that day does anything it reminds us
life is a joke covered in colorful paper   things that melt
burn   flowers   paint   sugar   things
that   never   last

a year after my brother's death   around day of the dead
the people from the pueblos my father worked with
    made a shrine for my brother

                     paper mache effigy
                     his little body
                     angel wings   a halo

my mother promptly destroyed it   making pueblo women cry
as my mother   the cruel   city woman   kicked the candles
threw the sugar skulls   with my brother's name on them
as far as she could

      both my parents have different stories

dad said you didn't go the funeral
   I went they dragged me I was numb
your father's sisters had to dress me they carried me to the car

dad said you never cried

                  I cried

          I never cried in front of him
         he cried because he wanted attention
I was busy asking why God would take my children away

dad says you have forgotten my brother and sister
  he says he will never forget them
            I know what your father says!
             he will never forget them
              because he likes pain
           he's a masochist or an idiot

           I have said goodbye to them
            because I loved them

              and love
             is letting go

     fucking sugar skulls

I remember the empty crib
I remember my mother not getting up from her bed
then some time later

my sister's death
  I grasp with 4-year-old hands my mother's wrist
as invisible things try
   to pull her away and take her with them

I remember   the lady at the sopes stand
in front of my mother asked me   how happy   I was
with my   new   sister?
   the look on my mother's face   ready to fall backwards
be swallowed up by a black hole   looked shocked when
I said   *happy, very happy,*
  I'm   happy   I   have   a   new   sister

   and we got our sopes   and we left
     how   tender   how   soft   strong
how   loving my mother's hand gripped mine
                              on our walk home

I guess I don't remember much of when
my   brother   and   sister   died
I must have been too young
                        good   my mother says

my father tells stories
when my brother in his crib was done with a bottle
he would throw it over his shoulder like a Viking
it would clang loudly on the floor   or he would
put the bottle through the bars with his baby hand
and drop it   letting the world know he was done

how can we let go
   if we have a day to bring back all the pain
      my mother says
don't you cry for me when I'm dead
not a tear   cry for me now
if you ever waste any money on flowers   for   me
when I'm dead   you will be the biggest fool!
   I like flowers now   when I'm alive!

go buy me some now   drop what you're doing and
go buy me some damn flowers
put them in an expensive vase
clean out my gutters   change all the light bulbs
and batteries in my smoke alarms
dust the high places I can't reach
take me out to dinner
enjoy me while I live darling
for when I'm dead I'll be dead
and I will not   be coming back   hijo

no matter how many candles
or pictures
    or flowers
   or songs

I'm not coming back.

GRATITUDE

I would like to thank Tomas Moniz, Roberto F. Santiago, James J. Siegle, and the Finishing School Writers Group who are so close to my heart; Joe Wadlington, Christina Ortega, Lark Omura, Zoe Young, Danae Barnes for reading the early drafts of this chapbook.

Thank you to Eugenia Chen, Tara Ramproot and Muni Diaries, Cassandra Dallet, MK Chavez, Judith Tannenbaum, Carrie Gocker, Matthew Beld, Sina Grace, and a very special thank you to Matthew James Decoster, Kevin Seaman, Bryan Borland and Sibling Rivalry Press, Evan Karp, Michelle Tea, Juliana Delgado Lopera, Virgie Tovar, Marga Gomez, Siouxsie Oki, Yo Ann Martinez and everyone at KQED, Dhaya Lakshminarayanan, Meliza Banales, Tony Valenzuela, everyone at Lambda Literary Foundation, everyone at *Foglifter*, Jyoti Arvey, Marcus Ewert, Alvin Orlof and everyone at Dog Eared Books Castro, Sarah Guerra, Anastacia Powers Cuellar and everyone at Brava Theatre, Pam Pennington and everyone at the Queer Cultural Center, and KB Tuffy Boyce with Queer Rebels for always supporting my writing.

ABOUT THE POET

Baruch Porras-Hernandez is a two-time winner of *Literary Death Match*, a regular host of poetry shows for KQED, and was named a Writer to Watch in 2016 by *7x7 Magazine*. His poetry can be found in several anthologies and journals such as Write Bloody Publishing's *Aim for the Head*, *The Tusk*, *Foglifter*, *Assaracus*, and many more. He has been an artist-in-residence at The Ground Floor at Berkeley Rep, a Lambda Literary Fellow in Poetry and in Playwriting, and was a Spoken Word resident artist at the Banff Center for the Arts in Canada. He is a recipient of grants from the San Francisco Arts Commission, Creative Work Fund, and Galería de la Raza. As a writer he has performed all over the place—NYC, LA, DC, parts of Canada, from *The Moth* to drag cabarets, from fancy universities to dark, damp caves. He was born in Mexico and lives in San Francisco.

ABOUT THE PRESS

Sibling Rivalry Press is an independent press based in Little Rock, Arkansas. It is a sponsored project of Fractured Atlas, a nonprofit arts service organization. Contributions to support the operations of Sibling Rivalry Press are tax-deductible to the extent permitted by law, and your donations will directly assist in the publication of work that disturbs and enraptures. To contribute to the publication of more books like this one, please visit our website and click *donate*.

Sibling Rivalry Press gratefully acknowledges the following donors, without whom this book would not be possible:

Tony Taylor
Mollie Lacy
Karline Tierney
Maureen Seaton
Travis Lau
Michael Broder & Indolent Books
Robert Petersen
Jennifer Armour
Alana Smoot
Paul Romero
Julie R. Enszer
Clayton Blackstock
Tess Wilmans-Higgins & Jeff Higgins
Sarah Browning
Tina Bradley
Kai Coggin
Queer Arts Arkansas
Jim Cory
Craig Cotter
Hugh Tipping
Mark Ward

Russell Bunge
Joe Pan & Brooklyn Arts Press
Carl Lavigne
Karen Hayes
J. Andrew Goodman
Diane Greene
W. Stephen Breedlove
Ed Madden
Rob Jacques
Erik Schuckers
Sugar le Fae
John Bateman
Elizabeth Ahl
Risa Denenberg
Ron Mohring & Seven Kitchens Press
Guy Choate & Argenta Reading Series
Guy Traiber
Don Cellini
John Bateman
Gustavo Hernandez
Anonymous (12)

www.ingramcontent.com/pod-product-compliance
Lightning Source LLC
Chambersburg PA
CBHW051704040426
42446CB00009B/1300